SUNRISE EXPRESS

by
Hank Ketcham

FAWCETT GOLD MEDAL • NEW YORK

A Fawcett Gold Medal Book
Published by Ballantine Books
Copyright © 1983 by Hank Ketcham
Copyright © 1980 by Field Enterprises, Inc.

Library of Congress Catalog Card Number: 83-90006

ISBN: 0-449-12787-7

Manufactured in the United States of America

First Ballantine Books Edition: September 1983
Third Printing: May 1984

"HI, MOM! I'M HOLDIN' **OPEN HOUSE!**"

"ARE YOU *SURE* THIS IS OUR CART?"

"I WONDER WHOSE BASKET I PUT ALL THAT STUFF IN...?"

PLAYIN' SCHOOL IS ABOUT AS DUMB AS PRACTICIN' GOIN' TO BED EARLY!"

"TROUBLE WITH SUMMER VACATION IS THERE'S NOTHIN' TO **DO**!"

"AT LEAST WE KNOW IT DON'T SAY **WET PAINT**."

"NO, MOM! I DIDN'T HAVE THE TANTRUM...
THE **SITTER** DID!"

"YA-YA-YA! I'M IN YOUR YARD!"

"AW, MR. WILSON... YOU'RE NO FUN ANY MORE."

"MY FOLKS DON'T BELIEVE IN SPANKIN'...
BUT THEY **SWAT** ONCE IN AWHILE."

"THE WORSTEST THING I EVER DID? TOOK A BATH, ATE ALL OF MY CARROTS AND THEN WENT TO BED EARLY, I GUESS."

"I'M JUST SINGIN' COMMERCIALS 'TIL I GET SLEEPY, DAD.
DON'T PAY NO ATTENTION."

"A DOG NEEDS ONE FLEA TO KEEP HIM HAPPY, DENNIS."

"YOU OUGHTA BE H'LARIOUS!"

"I MUST HAVE A BAD CONNECTION...HE **ALWAYS** FORGIVES ME!"

"HEY, WAIT A MINUTE! WE'RE GONNA HAVE TO LEAVE SOME OF THOSE CLOTHES HOME!"

"MR. WILSON SURE LOOKS DIFF'RUNT WHEN
HE'S HAPPY, DON'T HE?"

"CAN WE STICK AROUND 'TIL DARK, DAD? I WANNA
SEE 'EM ROLL UP THE SIDEWALKS!"

"THAT'S THE FIRST TIME I EVER ATE
SOMETHIN' THAT TRIED TO EAT ME FIRST!"

"NOW LET'S RIDE THE LITTLE AIRPLANES, DAD!"

"I FOUND IT LAYIN' ON TABLES IN ALL
THEM REST'RANTS WE ATE AT."

"T'S BUSY RIGHT NOW. OL' MARGARET'S STILL TALKING."

"ARE YOU GONNA TELL US ONE OF YOUR WILD STORIES, MR. HARRIS?"

"I GOTTA BE CAREFUL...THE OTHER NIGHT I ATE A CHICKEN LEG WITH MY DAD'S NAME ON IT."

"HE WOULDN'T **BITE** YA, MR. WILSON...YOU MUSTA BACKED INTO HIM WHILE HE WAS YAWNING!"

"GEE...STEAK **AGAIN**? CAN'T WE AFFORD **HOTDOGS** ONCE IN AWHILE?"

"YA KNOW...THAT WAS A PRETTY GOOD PARTY, ONCE IT GOT STARTED."

"AREN'T WE LUCKY THAT CORN DON'T POP AFTER WE EAT IT?"

"DENNIS... **GO HOME!**"

"I CAN TAKE A HINT."

"SEE? EVERYBODY **PAID** FOR WHAT THEY ATE...
AND HERE'S THE TWELVE CENTS!"

"ALL I'M ASKIN' FOR IS **JUSTISS**!"

"THEN HOW 'BOUT A LITTLE **MERCY**?"

"MARGARET SAYS MOTHER NATURE CAN **TALK** TO US, DENNIS!"

"YEAH. I'LL BET SHE'S SAYIN', 'GET OFF THE GRASS!'"

"THAT'S WHY THEY CALL HER **MOTHER** NATURE, JOEY...SHE KEEPS CHANGIN' HER MIND."

"THAT WAS THE MOST DEPRESSING PLACE I EVER SEEN!"

"STACY'S BACK-TO-SCHOOL SALE."

"THEN THE KID SAYS, 'IT WORKS JUST LIKE A WATER PISTOL, DON'T IT?' AND BEFORE I COULD GET IT AWAY FROM HIM..."

"THAT'S ME! DENNIS OCCUPANT."

"THE WILSONS ARE LOCKED OUT OF THEIR HOUSE, AND THEY'D LIKE *DENNIS* TO SHOW THEM HOW TO GET IN!"

"THANKS ANYWAY, DENNIS, BUT I DON'T **HAVE** A FAVORITE TUNE."

"ANOTHER REASON YOU SHOULDN'T SAY BAD WORDS, JOEY..
GOD HAS EVERYTHING **BUGGED**!"

"YEAH, MARGARET. I **KNOW**! BUT MY MOUTH IS SAYIN'
YUMMY SO LOUD I CAN'T HEAR MY TEETH SAYIN',
'DON'T DO IT!'"

"AW, MOM... NOT TODAY! I JUST GOT ALL MY STUFF ORGANIZED IN HERE!"

"LEMONADE AN' CHOCKLIT CAKE! DIDN'T I *TELL* YA THIS WAS THE BEST NEXT-DOOR IN THE WHOLE WORLD, JOEY?"

"MMMM... THEY SMELL LIKE *MUSTARD*."

"THAT'S **ME**! I HAD A HOTDOG FOR LUNCH."

"DON'T TAKE IT PERSONAL... HE FALLS ASLEEP
WATCHIN' TV AND READIN', TOO!"

I CAN'T PAY ATTENTION RIGHT AWAY WHEN SCHOOL STARTS. IT TAKES ME 'BOUT A WEEK TO GET SUMMER OUTA MY HEAD."

"I'M WITH **HER**."

"SORRY ABOUT THAT."

"THANK YOU FOR THE MEAT AN' THE POTATOES AN' THE BREAD...
AN' IF I DON'T MENTION THE CARROTS, I KNOW YOU'LL
UNDERSTAND."

"THAT'S THE WORST THING ABOUT GETTIN' OLD, JOEY...
YA START GETTIN' INNERESTED IN GIRLS!"

"MR. WILSON WROTE A SONG JUST FOR **ME**!"

"THERE'S NO-O-O PLA-A-CE LIKE *HOMEMMMMM*..."

"FOREVER? WELL, FOREVER IS LIKE A WHOLE **PLATE FULL** OF CREAMED CARROTS, JOEY."

"SORRY TO WAKE YA UP SO EARLY, MR. WILSON, BUT I WANTED
TO SHOW JOEY HOW YOU SLEEP IN A **TENT**!"

" IT'S **YOUR** SCIENCE
PROJECT, MARGARET..."

"**YOU** SIT ON THE EGG!"

"MR. WILSON SAYS EVERY CAT HAS HIS NIGHT, AND I GUESS LAST NIGHT MUSTA BEEN **HIS**!"

"TOO BAD THERE ISN'T A BUSTED
FINGERNAIL FAIRY, HUH, MOM?"

"ITS A COMBINASHUN SAMWICH. WANTA BITE?"

"HORSE RADISH AN' MUSTARD, MOSTLY."

"YEAH. **OLD** FOLKS ARE FUNNY ABOUT STUFF LIKE THAT.... TAKE *MINE*, F'RINSTANCE..."

"OW 'BOUT SOME PEPPY MUSIC TO SCRUB FLOORS BY ?"

"...AN' I'LL FEED THE PUPPIES! AN' SWEEP THE FLOOR! AN', IF YA WANT, I'LL EVEN *LIVE* HERE! I'M NOT GETTIN' ALONG TOO HOT AT HOME..."

"HIS IS THE KIND OF SHOES THEY WEAR. AN' *THAT'S* WHY YOU
OULDN'T OUGHTA NEVER LET A HORSE STEP ON YOUR FOOT!"

"SEE, JOEY...I **TOLD** YA SUMMER IS OVER!"

"WHAT SHOULD I TELL YOUR HUNGRY HUSBANDS WHEN THEY CALL UP?"

"I BETTER TELL YOU 'IT WAS A NICE PARTY' **NOW**, IN CASE YOU'RE NOT FEELIN' SO GOOD BY THE TIME I GO HOME."

"E **WERE** GOIN' TO THE MOVIES,
T WE DON'T HAVE ANY MONEY."

"DIDN'T I TELL YA MR. WILSON
WAS A GREAT GUY?"

"THAT'S NOTHIN'... **MY** MOM TORE A
BUMPER RIGHT OFF A TRUCK ONCE !"

"I DON'T *HAVE* A FAV'RITE KID', DENNIS."

"I'M AVAILABLE!"

"YOUR HEADACHE MUST BE CATCHIN'... MR. WILSON'S GOT ONE, T

"WHEN YOU LIVE NEXT DOOR TO A **VOLCANO**, YOU GOTTA EXPECT A FEW RUMBLES ONCE IN AWHILE."

"LET'S JUST SAY THIS WASN'T MY DAY, JOEY."

"HE'S NOT JUST BARKIN'...HE'S TALKIN' LONG-DISTANCE TO SOME OTHER DOG."

"A BUBBLE PIPE ISN'T HAZ'RDOUS TO YOUR HEALTH AS LONG AS YOU DON'T **INHALE** !"

"THERE'S NOTHIN' WRONG WITH MY APPETITE THAT A BOWL OF CHILI COULDN'T FIX."

"SHE'S COOKIN' LIVER AND CABBAGE
YOU WANTA COME WITH ME?"

YOUR ENGLISH IS **TERRIBLE!**"   "WANTA HEAR MY **CHINESE?**"

"I LOVE YOU, MOM .... THAT'S WHAT I *SHOULDA* SAID INSTEAD OF "SO WHAT?""

"IF YOU WANTA STAY ON HER GOOD SIDE, DON'T MAKE UP ANY DUMB JOKES ABOUT CHRISTOPHER COLUMBUS!"

"PSST...MOM?...CAN A TOASTER HAVE A NERVISS BREAKDOWN

"IF I EVER SAID YOUR PLACE WAS
IN THE KITCHEN ...FORGET IT!"

"YOU NEVER CAN TELL...IT'S SCARY. ONE DAY YOU'RE A ONLY CHILD AN' THE NEXT DAY YOU COULD HAVE THREE SISTERS!"

"IF WE **DO** BUY THIS HOUSE, WHICH CORNER WILL I BE SITTING IN?"

"BUT HE'S BAWLIN' SOMEBODY OUT...
AN' I DON'T THINK IT'S **ME!**"

"MOM? IS IT OKAY IF SOME OF THE KIDS COME TO MY HALLOWEEN PARTY A LITTLE EARLY?"

"JUST CHECKIN' ON WHAT'S FOR DINNER."

"OKAY, GINA...SPOIL MY APPETITE!"

"IT'S MARGARET. SHE WANTS TO TALK TO YOUR SICK FERN."

"I HAVEN'T GOT **TIME** TO BE SICK! THE OTHER GUYS WILL GET AHEAD OF ME WITH WHATEVER THEY'RE DOING!"

"HI, MR. WILSON! CAN I COME OVER IF I DON'T GET NEAR ANYTHING?"

"THIS IS SURE BETTER THAN SHOPPIN' WITH MOM! I LIKE STUFF YOU CAN GET YOUR **HANDS** ON!"

"GOOD NEWS, DAD! OUR BATHTUB IS STOPPED UP AND THE PLUMBER CAN'T COME FOR TWO DAYS!"

"WILL YOU STOP YELLIN' AT ME FOR A MINUTE, MR. WILSON? I CAN'T HEAR WHAT MY MOM IS YELLIN' AT ME!"

"...AND THANKS A LOT. AMEN."

"HE SAID NOT TO WORRY...HE WAS THE SAME WAY WHEN HE WAS MY AGE."

"WE DON'T CARE **WHAT** IT COSTS! **FIX IT!**"

"WITH **HIM** IT'S TRICK-OR-TREAT ALL YEAR LONG! WHY DOESN'T HE TAKE THE DAY **OFF**?"

"If I wasn't wearin' my
new suit . . . '

'What the heck . . . it's gonna
my OLD suit one of these day

"...AND THAT'S HOW WE PAY THE COST OF GOVERNMENT SERVICES."

"LIKE I WAS SAYIN', JOEY... TACKSES IS LIKE A WHOLE BOX OF TACKS."

"WAIT A SEC! BEFORE YOU ANSWER THE PHONE, LET ME TELL YOU **MY** SIDE OF IT!"

"I DON'T KNOW HOW IT WORKS, BUT MY DAD KEEPS TURNIN' IT **DOWN** TO SAVE MONEY AND MY MOM KEEPS TURNIN' IT **UP** TO GET WARM."

"WHILE YOU'RE REARRANGIN' STUFF, HOW ABOUT MOVIN' THE REFRIGERATOR IN **HERE**?"

"IF YA DON'T LIKE DUCKS OR BOATS OR EVEN BUBBLES...
WHATTA YOU **DO** WHILE YOU'RE SOAKIN'?"

"YA DON'T OFTEN FIND TWO STORKS LANDIN' AT THE SAME TIME!"

" 'LITTLE PITCHERS GOT BIG EARS' MEANS THEY'RE TALKIN' ABOUT SOMETHING **JUICY**."

'IF I FORGOT WHAT I DID, AND **YOU** FORGOT WHAT I DID, WHAT'S THE USE OF ME SAYIN' I'M SORRY I **DID** IT?'

'AM I GETTIN' **BIGGER** OR ARE THE CARS GETTIN' **SMALLE**

OH, GOOD! I BEEN WONDERIN' WHERE I LEFT THOSE NAILS!"

"I BETTER CALL YOU BACK, JOEY....IT GOT AWFUL **QUIET** AROUND HERE ALL OF A SUDDEN."

"UT YOU **SAID** WE COULD HAVE OUR QUICK-DRAW CONTEST ACK HERE!"

" JUST LOOK AT THAT! THEY SURE DON'T MAKE COWBOYS AS TOUGH AS THEY **USED** TO ! "

"STAND BACK...HE'S GONNA **EXPLODE**!"

"CAN WE GO OUT TO DINNER TONIGHT? ELSE WE'LL BE ARGUIN' OVER LEFTOVERS OF THE STUFF WE ARGUED ABOUT LAST NIGHT."

"IT STILL NEEDS *SOMETHING* ...BUT I
DON'T THINK WE GOT ANY OF IT."

"REMEMBER ME? I HAD ON MY **REGULAR** CLOTHES WHEN YOU CAME TO VISIT AT OUR HOUSE."

"THIS IS WHERE I'D PLUG IN MY 'LECTRIC BLANKET...IF MY FOLKS WEREN'T SO **MEAN**."

"MAYBE WE COULD GET A LOAN FROM THE GOVER'MENT."

"NAW...ONE OF 'EM WORKS IN THE BANK AND THE OTHER ONE HELPS OUR PLUMBER."

"MR. WILSON SAYS TURKEYS CELEBRATE THANKSGIVING *TOMORROW*."

HE THINKS IT'S HIS
CAT DINNER."

"WE DECIDED TO HAVE
CHILI INSTEAD."

" IT MUST BE FUN TO BREAK STUFF AND NOT
HAVE ANYONE **YELL** AT YOU."

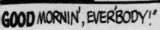

"THERE'S A LOTA *EXPERTS* HERE, IN CASE YOU'RE WONDERIN' IF YOU STILL GOT YOUR TOUCH."

"Do you know how much liver costs a **POUND**?"

"He says you was *ROBBED*."

"BEFORE I HANG UP, THANK YOU FOR THE QUARTER I FOUND TODAY. IT CAME IN REAL HANDY."

E'S **ALL BOY**, THAT'S
LL, ALICE."

"YOU **KNOW** I CAN'T TAKE
HIM TO THE OFFICE WITH ME!"

"IF MARGARET WAS HERE, WE COULD GET TO THE PLACE WHERE MY MOM SAYS 'OH, NO!'"

HY ASK **HER** ABOUT SANTA CLAUS? SHE DON'T
LIEVE IN NOTHIN' BUT *WOMEN'S LIP!*"

"THERE'S NO TRICK TO GETTIN' YOUR CHRISTMAS SHOPPIN'
DONE EARLY WHEN YOU ONLY GOT A **DOLLAR** TO SPEND."

"WHAT HAS CHRISTMAS GOT TO DO WITH **MONEY**?"

"I DON'T KNOW IF I SAID SOMETHIN' REAL **DUMB** OR REAL **SMART**."

"YOU CAN'T DO MUCH WITH A DIME THESE DAYS...I BETTE[R]
GIVE YA THE WHOLE FOURTEEN CENTS.'

"ALL HE WANTS TO TALK ABOUT IS THE **WEATHER!**'

"YOU *GOTTA* BELIEVE SANTA IS WATCHIN' YOU, JOEY ... OTHERWISE YOU'RE JUST BEIN' GOOD FOR **NOTHIN'**!"